FLOWERS AND FLORAL

COLORING BOOK

STRESS RELIEVING PATTERNS
ADULT COLORING BOOKS

COLOR TEST PAGE

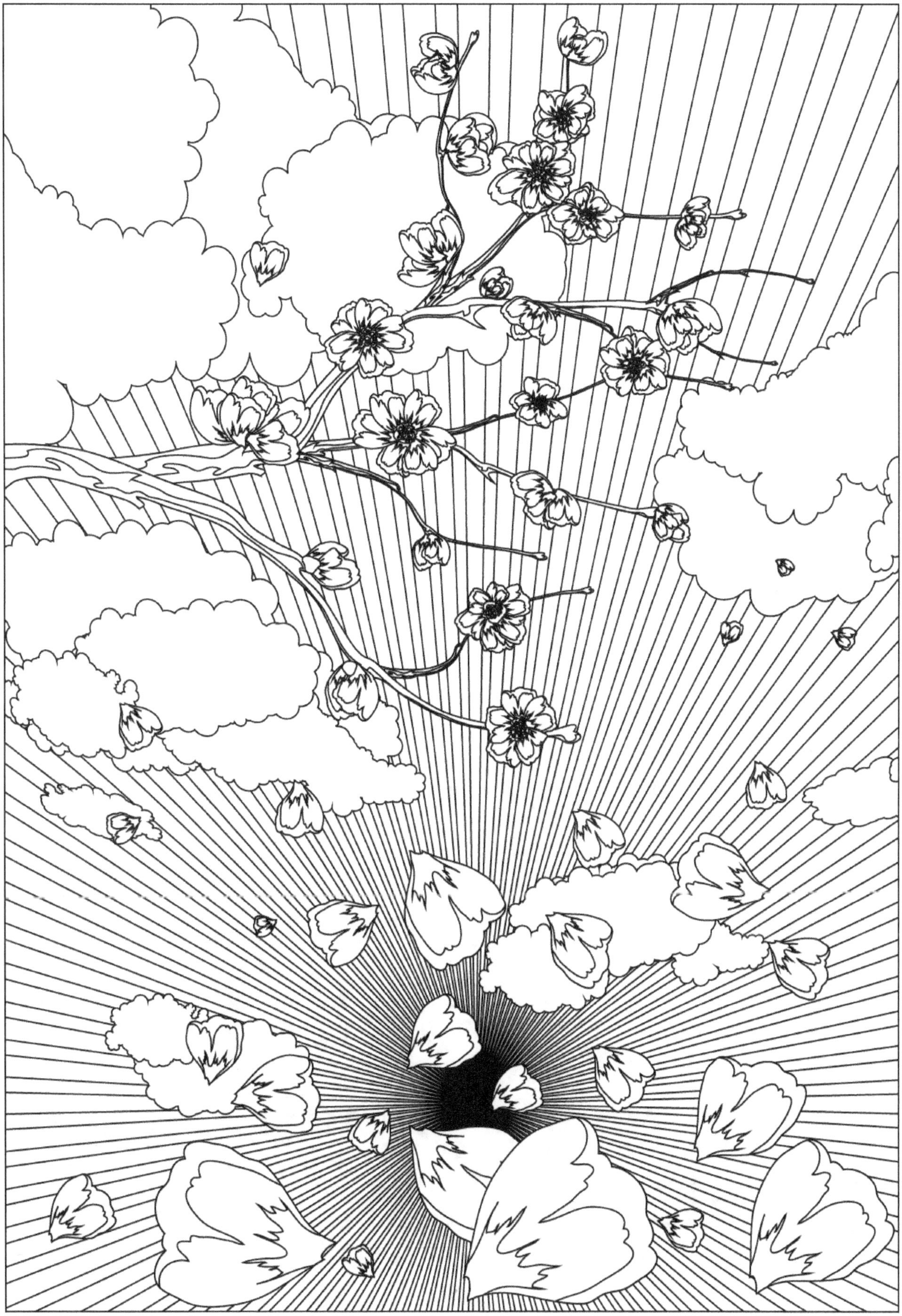

www.ingramcontent.com/pod-product-compliance
Lightning Source LLC
Chambersburg PA
CBHW081122280526
45787CB00007B/2941
* 9 7 8 1 5 3 5 2 4 5 6 1 6 *